Top Dog

The American Pit Bull Terrier

by William R. Sanford and Carl R. Green

CRESTWOOD HOUSE

New York

CIP

LIBRARY OF CONGRESS CATALOGING IN PUBLICATION DATA

Sanford, William R. (William Reynolds)
  American pit bull terrier

  (Top dog)
  Includes index.
  SUMMARY: Discusses the history, physical characteristics, care, and breeding of the American pit bull terrier, an extremely strong dog known for its willingness to fight.
  1. American pit bull terrier — Juvenile literature. [1. American pit bull terrier. 2. Dogs.] I. Green, Carl R. II. Title. III. Series: Sanford, William R. (William Reynolds), Top dog.
SF429.A72S36   1989   636.7'55 — dc20   89-31072
ISBN 0-89686-447-2

PHOTO CREDITS

Cover: Animals Animals: Robert Pearcy
Animals Animals: (Robert Pearcy) 13; (Zig Leszczynski) 19;
    (Jerry Cooke) 34; (John Lemker) 37
Sports Illustrated: (Lane Stewart) 4, 10, 15, 23, 24, 26, 31
    (Phil Huber) 21
Reynolds Photography: (Larry Reynolds) 9, 45

Copyright © 1989 by Crestwood House, Macmillan Publishing Company

Macmillan Publishing Company
866 Third Avenue
New York, NY 10022
Collier Macmillan Canada, Inc.

CRESTWOOD HOUSE
Produced by Carnival Enterprises

Printed in the United States of America

First Edition

10 9 8 7 6 5 4 3 2 1

TABLE OF CONTENTS

FOR MORE INFORMATION

For more information about American pit bull terriers, write to:

United Kennel Club
100 East Kilgore Road
Kalamazoo, MI 49001

National American
   Pit Bull Terrier Club
P.O. Box 756
Tenaha, TX 75974

WILL CLANCY BITE ME?

Jeremy White ran out of the farmhouse when he heard the sound of the car horn. In the driveway, a white station wagon was pulling to a stop. When he reached the car, Jeremy took one look inside and backed away. "I didn't come all the way to Ohio to ride with a pit bull," he declared. "Those dogs are dangerous!"

Tony Thorpe leaned out of the car. "Wait a minute," he told his new friend. "You don't need to be afraid. Clancy's the quietest, best-behaved dog in the world."

Tony's father climbed out and stood next to Jeremy. "Tony's right," he said. "You can take my word as a *veterinarian*. I wouldn't keep a vicious dog in my home."

Jeremy trusted Dr. Thorpe, but he wasn't convinced. "Clancy looks just like the pit bull that was on the news last year," he said. "I saw that dog try to kill an animal-control officer."

"A bad owner can turn almost any dog into a killer," the vet said. "More people are bitten

The pit bull terrier, which has been around for 200 years, was bred to fill a special need.

by German shepherds than are bitten by pit bulls. The problem is that American pit bull terriers, to give Clancy his proper name, are so terribly strong. If one gets it into its head to attack, it can do a lot of damage."

Dr. Thorpe reached in and grabbed Clancy's leash. The eager dog jumped out of the car and stood by the vet's side. Jeremy had to admit the dog's soft brown eyes didn't look very mean.

All at once, the pit bull pulled hard on his leash. Jeremy turned to see what was attracting the dog. All he saw were his uncle's cattle, grazing in a nearby field.

Tony had joined them. "Clancy gets excited when he sees cows," he said. "It's in his blood, my dad says."

Dr. Thorpe picked up the story. "Back in the 1300s, butchers used Clancy's bulldog ancestors to help them slaughter cattle. When the butcher gave the order, his dog grabbed a cow by the nose. While the bulldog hung on to keep the cow from running, the butcher killed it."

"What if Clancy slips his leash and goes after those cows?" Jeremy asked. He was still a little worried.

"He's been trained to leave cows alone," Tony assured him.

Jeremy had another thought. "I've heard that some people still *breed* pit bulls for fighting," he said. "Is that true?"

"I'm afraid so," Dr. Thorpe said with a sigh. "Dogfighting goes back to the ancient Romans. They enjoyed a sport called bearbaiting or bullbaiting. The bear or bull was tied to a long rope, and the dogs were turned loose to attack the animal."

"That's terrible," Jeremy said.

"People can do terrible things," Dr. Thorpe agreed. "At one time, there was a belief that a bull's blood was poison. That's why they wanted the bull to die while fighting with a dog. The violence was supposed to get rid of the poison. Butchers who sold meat that hadn't been 'baited' were fined."

"When did that sort of thing stop?" Tony asked his dad.

"England outlawed all of the blood sports in 1835," Dr. Thorpe answered. "That included dogfighting. What's more, dogfighting is illegal in all fifty states of the United States."

At last Jeremy reached down to pet Clancy's head. To his surprise, the dog licked his hand. "Hey, maybe Clancy and I will be friends after all," he said with a smile. "American pit bull terriers are interesting dogs. I want to learn more about them."

THE HISTORY OF THE PIT BULL TERRIER

Scientists classify the pit bull and all other dogs as meat-eating mammals. This places them in the order *Carnivora*. Next, dogs belong to the *Canidae* family. Other members of this family include wolves, foxes, and jackals. Finally, all domestic dogs belong to the same species, *Canis familiaris*.

Over the centuries, breeders have created dogs as different as the tiny Chihuahua and the giant wolfhound. Some breeds were known in ancient times, while others were created in this century. The pit bull terrier has been around for about 200 years. Like so many dogs, it was bred to fill a special need.

Toward the end of the 1700s, bullbaiting and dogfighting were popular sports. Everyone was looking for the perfect fighting dog. British breeders liked the bulldog's strength and courage, but they wanted a dog with a longer jaw and quicker reactions. They found those qualities by crossing the bulldog with the English terrier. In the early 1800s, the new breed

The American Staffordshire terrier is a close cousin of the pit bull.

was known as the bull-and-terrier. Later, because of its success in the dogfighting *pits*, it became the pit bull terrier.

The pit bull was first and foremost a fighting dog. Along with bullbaiting and dogfighting, the dog was a skillful rat catcher. Finally, in 1835, when all blood sports were outlawed, dogfighting went underground. In Staffordshire, the miners kept their pit bulls. They bred them for their fighting qualities. Dogs that didn't measure up were killed. Those fighting dogs were the ancestors of England's Staffordshire bull terrier.

Pit bulls can be good family pets.

Like the British, Americans used the earliest pit bulls for bearbaiting and dogfighting. When breeders tried to register their pit bulls with the American Kennel Club (AKC) in the late 1800s, they were turned down. The AKC refused to register fighting dogs. A breeder named C. Z. Bennett decided to set up the United Kennel Club (UKC) to register *purebred* pit bulls. The UKC gave the breed its name: the American pit bull terrier.

Pit bulls quickly adapted to a new role as

family pets. During the first part of this century, they were America's favorite dog. President Teddy Roosevelt kept a pit bull in the White House. Later, during World War I, a pit bull named Stubby helped capture a German spy. When movies became popular, a white pit bull starred in the "Our Gang" comedies. Even today, people laugh at Pete's clever clowning on TV reruns of "Our Gang."

In 1936, the AKC finally accepted the pit bull as a purebred. By now the American pit bulls had developed into a larger breed than their English cousins. Even so, the AKC insisted on using the name Staffordshire bull terrier. The word "pit" was dropped because it reminded people of dogfighting. In 1973, the AKC changed the name again, to American Staffordshire terrier.

A "Staff" is the AKC-registered cousin of the American pit bull terrier. The two breeds are look-alikes, and some dogs are registered with both the AKC and the UKC. The difference is that the Staff has been bred for show. It is a sweet-tempered, nonaggressive dog. American pit bull terriers, however, have been bred for *gameness*. The breed's admirers define gameness as a dog's willingness to fight to the death. Even though most owners do not fight their dogs, they prize this quality. If a pit bull is not properly trained, it can be a dangerous neighbor.

A CLOSE LOOK AT THE PIT BULL

Pit bulls are medium-sized dogs. Because they're broad and athletic, they seem bigger than they really are. Adult males stand 17 to 19 inches at the *withers* (the top of the shoulder). Females are about an inch shorter. From chest to rump, a pit bull's length should be equal to its height. Average males weigh about 35 pounds. Females weigh in at five pounds less. Pit bulls that are bred for size can grow as large as 65 pounds.

A healthy dog's hair is short, glossy, and stiff to the touch. Most colors are acceptable to breeders. Some dogs are all one color, but many are mixed, with patches of color. Showing an all-white or almost-all-white dog is discouraged. Black-and-tan or liver-colored dogs are equally undesirable. A pit bull's skin fits snugly. Only around the neck and chest will you see a few folds in the skin.

The hair of some pit bull terriers is all one color. Other dogs have coats with patches of different colors.

Pit bulls have large heads with deep, broad skulls. The *muzzle* is wedge shaped—rounded on top, but flattened below the eyes. The dark, round eyes are set wide apart and low in the skull. The nose is black and flat. The cheek muscles are large and bulge out above the powerful jaw. A pit bull's ears are set well back on the head. Some dogs hold their ears erect, while others let the upper half flop over.

The sharp teeth of a *carnivore* show clearly when a pit bull opens its mouth. After the baby teeth fall out, 42 adult teeth replace them. The upper jaw holds six *incisors* (for cutting) and two long *canines* (for holding and tearing). Behind these teeth are 12 *molars* and *premolars* (for slicing and crushing). The lower jaw has the same number of teeth in front, but contains two extra molars. If the dog is properly fed, a pit bull seldom develops cavities.

You can see the pit bull's strong jaws and sharp teeth at work when it's given a large steak. First, the dog tears off big chunks of meat with its incisors and canines. Next, it turns its head to the side and slices the meat into smaller chunks with its sharp molars. Chunks of food that would choke a human slide down the dog's elastic throat with ease.

At rest, the pit bull holds its head high on its short neck. The *forelegs* are straight, with the upper joint (the elbow) held close to the body. Similarly, the well-muscled hind legs do not turn inward or outward. The pit bull is a power runner, but it's also quite agile. Like other dogs, it has three *gaits*. When it's walking, only one foot leaves the ground at a time. In the trot, the right front and left rear feet move first, followed by the left front and right rear feet. When shifting into a gallop, the pit bull springs forward off its hind legs and lands

14 *The pit bull terrier's lean, muscular body makes it a fast and powerful runner.*

on its outstretched front legs. As it bounds ahead, the hind legs reach forward for the next high-speed thrust. The dog gallops with its head thrust forward and uses its tail like a rudder for balance. With all senses alert, the pit bull is ready for any adventure that comes its way.

THE PIT BULL'S KEEN SENSES

Dog experts believe the pit bull is one of the most intelligent of all dogs. Pit bulls learn quickly and seldom forget what they've been taught. You should not expect pit bulls to think like humans, however. A human brain weighs about three pounds. By contrast, a pit bull's brain weighs only about three ounces. Most of the dog's brain handles the tasks of seeing, hearing, and smelling.

A pit bull's view of the world is far different than yours. Dogs are colorblind, and their close-up vision is poor. They make up for that with fair distance vision and excellent night vision. The faintest gleam of light is enough to activate the light-sensitive cells on the dog's *retina.* A third eyelid, called the *haw,* closes when the eye is in danger.

Dogs see movement better than they do shapes. In one study, a dog's master was placed 250 yards away and told to stand still. A wooden cutout of the man's shape was set up nearby. When the dog was released, it ran toward the cutout! Only at a hundred yards did the animal hesitate. It was clearly confused. Finally, it picked up its master's scent and rushed to his side.

On the hunt, this isn't much of a problem. The game animals that dogs chase are usually moving. If a pit bull is chasing a rabbit, it will follow its prey right into the rabbit's burrow. As hunters say, the dog "goes to earth." That ability is inborn, thanks to the pit bull's terrier heritage ("terrier" comes from the Latin word *terra,* for "earth"). Only the fact that a pit bull can't squeeze into a rabbit hole keeps it from catching its prey.

A pit bull's eyesight may be limited, but its hearing is far better than yours. The human ear cannot hear high-pitched tones above 20,000 cycles a second. A dog can hear tones as high as 40,000 cycles a second and above. That's why a dog answers the call of a "silent" dog whistle. A pit bull also is better at locating the source of a sound. In one test, a dog was trained to "point" to the sound made by a buzzer. Then the dog was put inside a circle of 60 wooden planks. By remote control, the buzzer would sound from behind the planks, one at a time. Each time it did so, the dog went at once to the source of the sound.

If humans depend largely on their eyes, pit bulls depend mostly on their noses. Humans have about 5 million nerve endings to register smells. Pit bulls have 150 million! As the dogs breathe, molecules in the air register as scents. To the dogs, these stand out as clearly as billboards to our eyes. Dogs can be trained, for example, to sniff out small leaks in a gas pipeline. They find the leaks even when the pipe is a yard or more under the pavement.

A pit bull's senses of taste and touch are less developed. Dog food makers know that the smell of their products is more important than the taste. Because pit bulls will fight even when they're badly wounded, some people think they don't feel pain. That's not true. Like football players, fighting dogs are conditioned to ignore their pain.

A pit bull terrier's muzzle is rounded on top and flattened below the eyes.

IS THE PIT BULL THE DOG FOR YOU?

An old joke says that dogs and their owners tend to look alike. That's a funny thought, but it's not really true. Each breed of dog has its own look and personality. Some dogs are gentle, some are bold, and some are stubborn. The goal is to match the dog to the owner.

With that rule in mind, what type of person is attracted to the pit bull? Well, Sir Walter

Scott (a famous British writer), Thomas Edison (a great inventor), and Jack Dempsey (a heavyweight champion) all owned pit bulls. Maybe they liked the pit bull because it is so strong, both in body and in spirit.

It's possible that pit bulls are becoming too headstrong. In recent years, they've made some scary headlines. In 1986-1987, for example, dogs caused 18 deaths in the United States. Twelve of those deaths were blamed on pit bulls. The bites of most dogs are serious, but a pit bull's bite can be deadly. Its *instincts* tell it to bite down hard and to hold on. If it's driven off, it comes back again and again. Police officers say the only way to stop a pit bull is to shoot it.

The breed's fans argue that only a handful of the country's 500,000 pit bulls are dangerous. As one breeder says, "My dogs are babies. They'll lick you to death." She blames the pit bull attacks on insecure owners. These are people who keep savage dogs because it makes them feel more powerful. Pit bulls trained for dogfighting also can turn savage. To make matters worse, drug dealers are using pit bulls to protect their hideouts.

The pit bull isn't a "killing machine with a hair trigger," as some have said. But you can make a dog mean with poor care and bad

Sometimes insecure owners train their pit bull terriers to bark, bite, and attack.

training. Pit bull owners must face this issue. These are not lapdogs. Pit bulls are not cut out for life in small apartments. The breed projects a sense of power and purpose, not cuteness. Given firm, loving owners and plenty of exercise, they make fine pets. They seldom bark. They're great guard dogs. The sight of a pit bull will quickly discourage most burglars.

How do you convince people your pit bull isn't a menace to the neighborhood? First, keep it restrained and inside a dog-proof fence. When you go for a walk, put your dog on a heavy leash. Most of all, train it to total obedience. Your pit bull must never be allowed to run loose while you're out walking. If it does become mean, it should be put to sleep at once.

You can also help people learn your dog's good points. Like all well-bred pit bulls, it's a loving, healthy, natural clown. It's obedient and easy to keep clean. Most of all, your pit bull is "one tough dog." No matter how great the pain and discomfort, it'll never give up. Hitched to a sled, it can outpull dogs that were bred to pull heavy loads.

The pit bull has many uses outside of its role as pet and guard dog. It makes a silent hunting dog. Pit bulls have been trained to herd

Well-trained pit bull terriers are loving, healthy, and natural clowns.

livestock and to kill swamp rats. Out in the country, they make fine all-around ranch dogs. As with all dogs, owning a good pit bull starts with choosing the right *puppy*.

CHOOSING THE RIGHT PIT BULL PUPPY

You've studied both sides of the pit bull issue. You want a healthy dog that's easy to train, likes children, and is a fine guard dog.

Most pit bull breeders are proud of their gentle, playful dogs.

To many people, that sounds like a pit bull. How can you be sure you choose the right puppy? Here are the most popular questions asked by buyers, and the experts' answers:

What is the difference between a pit bull and a Staff? Side by side, you probably can't tell an American pit bull terrier from a Staffordshire terrier. A typical pit bull has been bred for gameness, while the Staff has been bred for show. Pit bull owners say the Staff has lost most of its natural aggressiveness. Staff breeders, for their part, look down on the pit bull as an over-aggressive fighter. One solution is to buy a puppy that is registered by both the AKC and the UKC. These dogs meet AKC standards (as Staffs), but have kept some of their pit bull toughness.

Where can I find a good-quality puppy? Many families go to the nearest pet store when they want to buy a puppy. In the case of a pit bull, it's best to buy from a good breeder. First, breeders who really care about their dogs won't sell you a diseased or bad-tempered puppy. Second, by looking at the kennel's adult dogs, you can quickly see the type of dogs that are being bred there. Beware of pit bull breeders who boast about the "fighting qualities" of their dogs. You're looking for a pet, not a gladiator. Locate a good breeder by talking to some pit bull owners, or ask your local vet for advice. If that doesn't work, look up the names of breeders in *Dog World* (for Staffs) and *Bloodlines Journal* (for pit bulls).

How much will I have to pay? If you want to show an AKC-registered Staff, you'll have to pay around $600 for a top-grade dog. A pet-quality dog, by contrast, will cost about $300. The prices for pit bulls are similar, but the quality of the puppies varies greatly.

How do I pick one puppy out of a litter?

When you visit a kennel, look first at the puppy's parents. The adults should be handsome, friendly dogs. Next, study the *litter*. Look for bold, outgoing puppies. Pick one that keeps its confidence even when it's put down in a strange place. Now, examine the puppy carefully. A healthy puppy is alert, playful, and clean. Never buy a puppy that has cloudy eyes, a swollen belly, or a runny nose. Check the puppy's health record. Ask for a copy of the puppy's *pedigree*. You'll need these papers to register the dog with one of the kennel clubs. After you buy a dog, take it to your vet. If it fails the checkup, return it to the seller.

A healthy pit bull puppy should have clear eyes, a firm belly, and a clean nose.

Should I buy a male or a female puppy? How old should it be? Males tend to be larger and more aggressive. Females make better house dogs, and they give you the added option of raising puppies. Male or female, a pit bull can leave its mother when it's only six weeks old. Experts say it's better to wait another three weeks. Older puppies are fully *weaned* (they no longer nurse from their mothers) and have had their puppy shots. They're ready to go home with you to start their training.

TRAINING A PIT BULL PUPPY

Training a pit bull puppy is a delight and a challenge. If you've chosen well, your pit bull is alert, healthy, and playful. Right now, it's so cute and cuddly you hate the thought of scolding it. Control that impulse. An out-of-control pit bull can be dangerous. Right from the first day, make sure your dog knows you're the boss.

Every step in training a dog should follow the rule of the three p's: patience, persistence, and practice. Don't get upset if your dog doesn't learn something the first time. Give it the command over and over until it gets it right.

If you bought your pit bull from a good breeder, it already likes people. Play with it, talk to it, and take it with you on short trips. Remember, your pit bull is a dog, driven by its instincts. If you always use its name, it'll soon respond. Reward it when it does. A kind word and a friendly pat will make your puppy want to please you all the more.

You can start *housebreaking* your dog on the first day you bring it home. Start with one of its instinctive behaviors: It won't soil its own bed. To take advantage of that, fix up a kennel. A wire cage or a wooden crate will be fine. Your dog will accept the kennel as its den. It won't want to soil it, so you can control the times when it relieves itself. After your puppy is used to the kennel, you can use it as a travel case.

Your dog will usually relieve itself after eating. Feed it at the same times every day. Then take it outside to the spot you want it to use. The odors it leaves there will encourage it to use the spot again. You also can leave some slightly soiled newspapers by the back door. If someone forgets to take the dog outside, it'll use the papers because of the odor. That's a small victory, because you've got your dog as far as the door. Soon it'll be whining and scratching to remind you to let it out.

Never overlook a mistake. If you see your puppy soil the hall carpet, hold its nose close to the mess and scold it. Then take it outside. Later, use a strong cleaner to wash the soiled spot. Any odor left behind will draw the dog back to the same place. Punishing your dog "after the fact" won't do any good. If that happens, clean up the mess and go on with the regular training.

Any display of aggression must be handled at once. If your pit bull snarls at anyone, dog or human, scold it at once. Use a rolled-up newspaper and smack the ground next to it. If it's on a *choke chain,* pull back to cut off its air. When it relaxes, release the pressure. It must be taught that aggressive behavior is wrong. *Reinforce* these lessons with lots of pats and praises. Occasionally, when your dog does something right, pop a treat into its greedy mouth. It'll work even harder to please you.

At this point, your puppy is still in nursery school. It has many lessons yet to learn. Both of you are off to a good start, however. It isn't easy to turn a happy-go-lucky puppy into a well-behaved pet, but the payoff is worth it.

CARING FOR YOUR PIT BULL

Compared to a long-haired dog, caring for a healthy pit bull is quite simple. Simple doesn't mean easy, however. No one should own a dog unless he or she is ready to provide a good diet, regular visits to the vet, proper *grooming*, and exercise.

Some new dog owners buy fancy canned foods and lots of doggy treats. None of that is necessary. Like all dogs, the pit bull does best on a balanced diet that's heavy on protein. Most breeders use a good-quality dry dog food. They add a few drops of a vitamin-mineral mix to each bowlful. Dry food keeps the dog's teeth clean and is less likely to attract flies outdoors. Keep the dog's water bowl full at all times.

Growing puppies and pregnant females need extra protein. Your new puppy will eat five times a day, but at four months you can drop to three feedings a day. Two meals are enough for a nine-month-old dog, and at one year the adult dog can get by on one meal a day. Adding hamburger or raw meat to the dry food always improves a dog's appetite.

Any dog that sleeps outside needs a comfortable, rainproof doghouse.

What you don't feed your pit bull is also important. A dog should be slightly hungry after each meal. Given all the food it wants, your pit bull will grow fat and lazy. Feeding the dog from the table will turn it into a world-class beggar. Above all, never give fish or chicken bones to your dog. Dogs choke to death every day on small, splintery bones. Instead of sweets, give your dog a bonemeal treat now and then. Chewing on these tough "bones" exercises the jaws and keeps the dog's teeth clean.

If your pit bull sleeps outside, it will need shelter. Build a rainproof doghouse and shelter it from the wind. You don't have to invest in a

doggy "palace." A small doghouse holds in body heat and keeps the dog warmer. Be sure the bedding inside the doghouse is off the ground. Instead of buying a special pad, give your pit bull a bed of clean straw. If you can't get straw, use shredded newspapers and an old blanket.

The vet is an important person in your pit bull's life. All new puppies should begin life with a series of "puppy shots." These shots guard the dog from *distemper* and other serious diseases. The vet can also check for *worms* and skin problems. Worms are parasites that live in a dog's intestines. They're dangerous if left untreated, and only an expert should "worm" the dog. The vet will tell you if you're keeping the dog clean enough. A daily brushing and a bath once in a while will keep a pit bull's coat shining and healthy. Fleas are a problem for all dogs, and some pit bulls are allergic to flea bites. Keeping the dog and its bedding free of fleas will require a flea collar.

Finally, see that your pit bull has plenty of exercise. If you leave the dog outside, be sure the fence is at least six feet high. It should be set in concrete. Otherwise, a pit bull will either climb the fence or dig under it. Many owners keep their dogs tethered. The favorite *tether* is a long chain attached to a strong overhead cable. This setup allows the dog to move freely, but keeps it safely anchored in the yard. This freedom, plus a daily three-mile walk, will keep your dog in good condition. You can expect your pit bull to live for 12 to 15 years.

BREEDING A PIT BULL

One of the great truths of life is that most people love baby animals. Better yet, who can resist a litter of playful pit bull puppies? Their joy in living overflows their small bodies and infects everyone near them.

If your female is a purebred, you don't want her to give birth to *crossbred* puppies. You'll have to find a suitable mate for your *bitch* (as female dogs are called).

Your female should be at least 14 months old before you breed her. It's a good idea to have her checked by your vet before you begin. If your dog has any health problems, they should be corrected first. The vet will also tell you if your dog has any serious flaws that she might pass on to her puppies. In that case, it

would be best not to breed her.

If you want quality puppies, you'll have to find a champion male, or *stud*, for your female. Once you do, the stud's owner will expect you to pay a fee for the service. You can pay the stud fee in cash or you can give the owner "the pick of the litter." When all is ready, mark the calendar the next time your dog comes into *heat*. This means she's ready to mate. Take her to the stud between the tenth and fourteenth days. If she doesn't become pregnant, the stud's owner will let you bring her back during her next heat.

Pit bull puppies are born nine weeks after the female is mated. During that time, your dog will need special care. Give her a high-protein diet and lots of gentle exercise. Prepare a *whelping* box and set it up in a warm, quiet place. If your dog is used to sleeping in the box, she won't try to give birth under the sofa.

The great moment can arrive at any time after the sixtieth day. Most pit bull bitches give birth with little trouble. Her litter may have as few as four puppies or as many as 14! Each puppy emerges headfirst, covered in its birth sac. After the female helps it break the sac, she bites through the *umbilical cord*. Next, she licks the puppy to clean and warm it. After

Pit bull puppies grow quickly. When they are ten days old, their eyes open. At six weeks the puppies begin eating on their own.

she cleans each one, you can hold it to her *teat* to let it suckle. The puppies, which weigh about 12 ounces, arrive about 30 minutes apart.

Born deaf and blind, the puppies grow with amazing speed. At ten days, they'll have their eyes open. Four days after that, they'll be walking on wobbly legs. The mother will start weaning the puppies after four weeks, and by six weeks they'll be eating on their own. At ten weeks, there's another decision to make. Do you want the puppies' ears to stand up straight? If so, you'll have to have their ears *cropped* (trimmed).

Most breeders don't crop their dogs' ears, but others say that cropping gives a *show dog* an advantage. If you vote for cropping, make sure you live in a state where cropping is permitted. If you do, have it done by a vet who knows how to shape a pit bull's ears. If you can't make up your mind, wait and let the puppies' new owners make their own decisions.

DOGFIGHTING

In October 1988, two pit bulls escaped from a backyard in a California city. Free to wan-

Most pit bull owners prefer not to crop their dog's ears. They let the ears grow naturally.

der, they entered another yard and killed a neighbor's dog. The police were called. The officers saw the two pit bulls running toward a school and shot them. Maddened by the taste of blood, the pit bulls might have attacked the children at the school.

As so often happens, the dogs were shot because of their owner's mistakes. Pit bulls that are trained for guard duty and for dogfighting are naturally aggressive. Unless they're kept under tight security, they are dangerous. Dogfighting is illegal in all 50 states, but even so, dogfighting for money still goes on. The laws are often ignored. In some states, an owner who trains and fights a dog can be fined up to $50,000 and sent to jail. Both the AKC and the UKC have policies that oppose the fighting of dogs for fun, sport, or profit.

When dogfighting does take place, it is held in secret. Gamblers compare the bloodlines of the dogs and their past records. The fights take place in a pit that is about 16 feet square. A 30-inch wooden wall keeps the dogs in the pit. The floor is covered by an old carpet. The dogs' handlers must stay behind "scratch lines" marked by white tape.

The match begins with a signal from the judge. The pit bulls lunge at each other and the fight is on. Each dog takes its best hold and tries to throw its opponent. The fight continues until one dog is killed, jumps out of the pit, or gives up. At the end, the dogs are scarred and bloody. The handlers kill severely injured dogs to end their suffering. Other dogs are "put down" (killed) because they didn't fight hard enough.

Animal-rights groups around the United States are working to stop this illegal activity. Dogfighting, they say, is a form of cruelty to animals.

In recent years, a less violent form of competition has become popular. Pit bulls are now being entered in *weight-pulling contests*. The contests are exciting, and the dogs seem to enjoy themselves. Best of all, the owners can breed their dogs for strength and stamina. A weight-pulling pit bull doesn't need to be vicious or savage.

WHY DO SOME DOGS GET OUT OF CONTROL?

The sight is all too common. The dog scampers along, pulling its owner this way and that. It's a case of the dog taking the master for a walk. If the dog is a dachshund, the scene makes you laugh. If it's a pit bull, it can be a little scary.

Why do some dogs get out of control? This is an important question. A dog that won't obey its owner is a nuisance. Worse yet, the dog may be a danger to the entire neighborhood.

The Conans own a pit bull. Diesel was a

WITHDRAWN 39

playful, headstrong puppy. Now, he's grown up to be a powerful adult dog. Diesel's daily walk with Mr. Conan is a good example. Man and dog go where Diesel wants to go and stop when Diesel wants to stop. When they get home, Mrs. Conan complains that Diesel has been relieving himself in the house. Then, to top off a bad week, Diesel tries to bite the mail carrier.

The Conans can't control their own dog. What went wrong?

Some people would blame the problem on the fact that Diesel is a pit bull. That's not fair. This is an owner problem, not a pit bull problem. To put it simply, Diesel has taken over as the leader of the Conan "pack." Just like his wild ancestors, he was born to fight for the top job. Most dogs do this, but they lose the struggle. After all, humans are bigger and smarter than their dogs. In this case, Diesel won his battle with the Conans.

The family didn't plan it this way. In the puppy days, they thought Diesel was "terribly cute." They didn't have the heart to scold him. If he chewed on the rug, they begged him to stop by giving him a doggy bone. Rewarded for bad behavior, Diesel kept on behaving badly. The pit bull won the "battle of the bed," for example, by wearing down his owners. The

Conans put him in his own bed every night, but they didn't have the heart to lock him up. As a result, Diesel always ended up sleeping on the sofa. After a month, the family gave up. Now Diesel sleeps wherever he wants to sleep.

Giving Diesel his own way allowed him to take over the leadership of the pack. Now, as top dog, he thinks he's the dominant member of the family. When Diesel relieves himself in the house, it's not because he's forgotten his puppy training. Like any dominant male dog, he's marking his territory! When Diesel tries to bite a visitor, he's defending his pack against outsiders. In dog terms, his behavior is perfectly natural.

What can be done about Diesel's biting? The experts say the Conans don't have a choice. They *must* regain control. Mr. Conan must put Diesel on a choke chain. When he lunges at someone, Mr. Conan should yank on the chain and cut off the dog's air. At the same time, he should scold Diesel in a loud, firm voice. When Diesel does behave, he should be praised.

The Conans won't win this battle overnight. They must be tough and consistent. If they can't control Diesel, perhaps a dog trainer can do the job for them. Until he's under control, Diesel will never be anyone's "best friend."

PIT BULLS AREN'T LIKE OTHER DOGS

Remember this classic cartoon? A cat races across the yard and streaks up the nearest tree. An angry dog is one jump behind. When the dog reaches the tree, it skids to a stop. The cat is already safe, perched high in the tree. The cartoon dog barks a few times and then tries to saw down the tree.

If the dog were a real-life pit bull, the scene would play differently. Pit bulls climb trees! If there's something in the tree it wants, the dog will find a way to get it. Pit bulls are good climbers because they use their strong forelegs almost like arms. By gripping with their forelegs and pushing with their hind legs, they can scramble up a rough-barked trunk.

A pit bull named Chip spent a lot of time in trees. Bill, his owner, thought Chip liked the view from up there. The first time Bill saw Chip high in a tree, Bill nearly had an accident. Chip had climbed to the top of a tall tree

42

just before Bill was due home from work. When Bill drove up and saw Chip in the tree, he almost crashed through the garage door.

After a while, the neighbors got used to the sight of the tree-climbing dog. From his high lookout point, Chip kept tabs on the local cats. One day, Bill was standing in the alley behind the house, talking to a friend. All at once, they heard the ear-splitting screech of an angry tomcat. Twenty feet up, Chip was staring at the cat from his favorite branch.

"Well," Bill's friend laughed, "I never thought I'd see a pit bull treed by a tomcat." Chip had written a new ending to the old cartoon.

Like most dogs, pit bulls love to play. Being pit bulls, though, they sometimes overdo things. Ever since he was a puppy, Pat and his owners played tug-of-war. Even though Pat weighed only 45 pounds, very few people could win a tug-of-war with him. Pat would twist and turn until he tore the stick out of his opponent's hand. Then, holding the stick in his mouth, he'd prance around in a victory dance.

With his passion for sticks, Pat didn't always make friends. A visitor panicked one day when he saw Pat heading toward him. The man picked up a wooden stake and waved it over his head. He was warning the dog, but Pat thought the man wanted to play. Pat ran up the man's side and grabbed the stake. The man fell over and the dog landed on the ground with the stake in his jaws.

A local teenager bragged that he would have chased Pat away with the stake. Pat's owner invited him to try. The teenager swung the stake at Pat, who caught it in his teeth. The teenager yanked as hard as he could, but Pat twisted the stake from his hands with ease. Then the dog went into his happy victory dance.

Not all people have funny stories to tell about pit bulls. Many people believe the American pit bull terrier is dangerous. These people fight for rules to restrict pit bulls.

In 1989, New York City passed a law that said no new pit bulls would be allowed in the city after October 1. Owners who already had pit bulls would have to follow certain rules.

Owners of pit bulls in New York City must be at least 18 years old. When an owner takes his or her pit bull for a walk, the dog must wear a leash and muzzle.

Although many people are glad this law was passed, others think it is unfair to the dogs. One veterinarian said the owners were at fault, not the dogs. He said the owners teach their pit bulls to fight.

The American Staffordshire terrier, like its pit bull cousin, enjoys gnawing on a thick stick.

Not all pit bulls are mean and not all owners teach their pit bulls bad habits. Before you buy a pit bull, or any other type of dog, watch it closely. Any dog with aggressive habits should be kept in a secure area away from people.

▌GLOSSARY/INDEX

Bitch 33, 35—An adult female dog.

Breeding 7, 8, 11, 12, 22, 24, 25, 33, 35, 39— Mating a quality bitch to a quality male.

Canines 14—The four long, sharp fangs in the front of a dog's mouth.

Carnivore 13—A meat-eating animal.

Choke Chain 29, 41—A leash made from heavy metal links that is used in training a dog.

Crop 36, 37—To trim a dog's ears so they will stand up straight.

Crossbred 10, 11, 33—A dog whose parents are from different breeds.

Distemper 32—A serious disease that affects puppies.

Gait 14—The movements of a dog's feet when it's walking, trotting, or galloping.

Forelegs 14, 42—The front legs of an animal.

Gameness 11—The qualities of endurance and courage that are typical of pit bulls.

Grooming 30—Brushing an animal to keep its coat clean.

Haw 17—The dog's third eyelid.

Heat 35—The time when a bitch is ready to mate.

Housebreak 28—To train a puppy so it doesn't relieve itself inside the house.

Incisors 14—The sharp cutting teeth that grow

GLOSSARY/INDEX

at the front of the dog's jaw between the canines.

Instincts 20, 28—Natural behaviors that are inborn in a dog.

Litter 25, 26, 33, 35—A family of puppies born at a single whelping.

Molars 14—The dog's back teeth, used for slicing and crushing.

Muzzle 13, 19—The part of the head that includes the mouth, jaws, and nose of a dog.

Pedigree 26, 38—A chart that lists a dog's ancestors.

Pits 9, 38—The enclosed spaces in which dogfights are held.

Premolars 14—The dog's back teeth, used for slicing and chewing.

Puppy 23, 24, 25, 26, 27, 28, 29, 30, 32, 33, 34, 35, 36, 40, 43—A dog under one year of age.

Purebred 10, 11, 33—A dog whose ancestors are all of the same breed.

Reinforce 29—To give a dog a reward when it obeys a command.

Retina 17—The inner lining of the eyeball.

Show Dog 36—A dog that meets the highest standards of its breed.

Stud 35—A purebred male used for breeding.

▌GLOSSARY/INDEX